MAX AXIOM
AND THE SOCIETY OF SUPER SCIENTISTS

OCEAN PLASTICS PROBLEM

BY ELIZABETH PAGEL-HOGAN

ILLUSTRATED BY ERIK DOESCHER

CAPSTONE PRESS
a capstone imprint

Published by Capstone Press, an imprint of Capstone.
1710 Roe Crest Drive
North Mankato, Minnesota 56003
capstonepub.com

Library of Congress Cataloging-in-Publication Data
Names: Pagel-Hogan, Elizabeth, author. | Doescher, Erik, illustrator.
Title: Ocean plastics problem : a Max Axiom super scientist adventure / by Elizabeth Pagel-Hogan ; illustrated by Erik Doescher.
Description: North Mankato, Minnesota : Capstone Press, [2022] | Series: Max Axiom and the society of super scientists | Includes bibliographical references and index. | Audience: Ages 8–11 | Audience: Grades 4–6
Identifiers: LCCN 2021012673 (print) | LCCN 2021012674 (ebook) | ISBN 9781663921758 (paperback) | ISBN 9781663907516 (hardcover) | ISBN 9781663907486 (ebook PDF) | ISBN 9781663907509 (kindle edition)
Subjects: LCSH: Plastic marine debris—Environmental aspects—Juvenile literature. | Plastic marine debris—Environmental aspects—Comic books, strips, etc.
Classification: LCC TD427.P62 P34 2022 (print) | LCC TD427.P62 (ebook) | DDC 363.738--dc23
LC record available at https://lccn.loc.gov/2021012673
LC ebook record available at https://lccn.loc.gov/2021012674

Summary: Plastic is everywhere . . . even in our oceans! But how did it get there, why does it matter, and what can we do about it? In this nonfiction graphic novel, Max Axiom and the Society of Super Scientists go on an exciting, fact-filled mission to find out.

Editorial Credits
Editors: Abby Huff and Aaron Sautter; Designer: Brann Garvey; Media Researcher: Svetlana Zhurkin; Production Specialist: Laura Manthe

All internet sites appearing in back matter were available and accurate when this book was sent to press.

TABLE OF CONTENTS

THE SOCIETY OF
SUPER SCIENTISTS

MAX AXIOM

After years of study, Max Axiom, the world's first Super Scientist, knew the mysteries of the universe were too vast for one person alone to uncover. So Max created the Society of Super Scientists! Using their superpowers and super-smarts, this talented group investigates today's most urgent scientific and environmental issues and learns about actions everyone can take to solve them.

LIZZY AXIOM

NICK AXIOM

SPARK

THE DISCOVERY LAB

Home of the Society of Super Scientists, this state-of-the-art lab houses advanced tools for cutting-edge research and radical scientific innovation. More importantly, it is a space for Super Scientists to collaborate and share knowledge as they work together to tackle any challenge.

And there's even more plastic litter on the beach.

This all needs to be cleaned up before another animal gets trapped. Come on, Spark!

WOOF! WOOF!

Nick is going to have his hands full picking up so much plastic. But the bigger issue is how it got here in the first place.

You're right, Lizzy, and it's not just this beach. Plastic is found on beaches and in oceans all over the world.

While Nick's cleaning up, let's see what we can uncover about this plastic problem.

Look, Max! We're surrounded by plastic. It's in everything from sunglasses to cars, and even aircraft!

Plastic is a very useful material. It's strong and lightweight. It can be shaped into almost anything.

Plastic isn't a natural substance. Most plastic is made from oil, natural gas, or coal. It was invented in 1869 but wasn't used much until after World War II. Then it started taking off.

In 1950, people created 1.5 million tons of plastic worldwide. In 2018, we made more than 350 million tons!

TRAVELING DEBRIS

On March 11, 2011, a 9.0 magnitude earthquake struck off the coast of Japan. A tsunami followed. The disaster killed many people and caused billions of dollars in damage. It also washed an estimated 5 million tons of debris into the Pacific Ocean. Ocean currents carried the plastic debris from the earthquake. The first plastic to reach North America was a soccer ball that washed ashore in Alaska in March 2012.

Many people are looking for unique solutions to our plastic problem.

Dutch entrepreneur Boyan Slat was only 18 when he started The Ocean Cleanup.

The group invented a net-like device to catch floating plastic. It gets carried through the ocean by waves and wind. As it moves, a large U-shaped tube gathers plastic on the surface. Screens hang down to catch plastic in the water.

When the screens are full, the device sends a signal to the group to pick up the plastic. The device caught its first plastic in 2019.

The Ocean Cleanup and other groups have also invented systems that catch plastic in rivers before it enters the ocean.

PLASTIC TYPES

Not all plastic is recyclable. There are two main types of plastic: thermoset and thermoplastic. "Thermo" means heat. Thermoplastics can be melted and made into new products. Plastic bottles are thermoplastics. But thermoset plastics can't be recycled. Their polymer bonds won't change with heat. Plastic table tops and Formula 1 race cars are made from thermoset plastics.

TAKE ACTION!

Reducing plastic is a worldwide project. But you can start working on it now in your neighborhood.

- Plan ahead! Keep a reusable water bottle with you, have a set of utensils handy for on-the-go meals, and carry a reusable shopping bag.

- Don't trash plastic furniture or utensils. Donate them to a charity or a program like the Freecycle Network so others can use items you don't need anymore.

- Reuse plastic items for as long as you can. Clean plastic takeout containers and reuse them in your lunch. Grow plants in a plastic juice jug. Then water them with a watering can made from a clean plastic laundry detergent bottle.

- Get creative! Think of new uses for plastic items. Find out what plastics your town recycles. Make sure you always recycle those items.

- Write to your local government and ask them to help increase recycling in your schools and community. Encourage friends and neighbors to do the same.

- Start a poster campaign in your school or neighborhood. Teach people about why it's important to reduce, reuse, and recycle plastics.

- Pick up plastic in your neighborhood. If you can recycle it, do it! If not, cleaning up litter keeps it out of our streams, rivers, and oceans.

- When you are shopping, try to pick products with no packaging or recyclable packaging. If you can, shop at a farmer's market or community market. Buying local usually means less plastic packages.

- Try a plastic-free challenge! Can you go through a day without using plastic?

MORE PLASTIC FACTS

Some scientists think the plastic trash floating near the surface is only 1 percent of all the plastic in the ocean. It is also building up on the ocean floor. Recent studies discovered that there is more plastic on the ocean floor than is floating near the surface. The deepest piece of plastic was found in the Marianas Trench in 2018 at 36,000 feet (11 kilometers) deep!

Plastic is found around the world—even in places where humans don't live! Microplastics have been found in the snow in Antarctica. On uninhabited islands such as Milman Island near Australia, plastic is ruining what should be beautiful beaches. Sea turtle researchers collected more than 165 pounds (75 kg) of plastic from the shore.

Scientists and businesses are working on creative alternatives to plastics. One company in London is developing a plastic made from seaweed. This plastic is not only biodegradable—it's edible!

Scientists in Korea may have discovered a beetle larvae that can eat, digest, and break down a specific kind of plastic called polystyrene.

GLOSSARY

disposable (dih-SPOH-zuh-buhl)—made to be thrown away

gyre (JAHYUR)—a large system of rotating ocean currents

landfill (LAND-fil)—a place where garbage is buried

litter (LIH-tuhr)—trash that has been thrown on the ground or carelessly left somewhere

manta trawl (MAN-tuh TRAWL)—a netted device that is pulled through water to collect water samples

microplastic (mye-kroh-PLAS-tik)—a piece of plastic less than 0.2 inches (5 mm); microplastics can be made to be of small size or they are pieces that break off from large plastic

monomer (MAH-nuh-muhr)—a single molecule that can be linked to other molecules

plastic (PLAS-tik)—a strong, lightweight material created by people that can be formed into many shapes when heated and then set as it cools

pollutant (puh-LOOT-uhnt)—a material that can damage the environment

polymer (PAH-luh-muhr)—a group of many monomers linked together

recycle (ree-SYE-kuhl)—to make used items into new products

reduce (rih-DOOS)—to make something smaller in size or quantity

READ MORE

Howell, Izzi. *Pollution Eco Facts*. New York: Crabtree Publishing Company, 2019.

Hustad, Douglas. *Cleaning Up Plastic with Artificial Coastlines*. Minneapolis: Abdo Publishing, 2020.

Smith-Llera, Danielle. *Trash Vortex: How Plastic Pollution Is Choking the World's Oceans*. North Mankato, MN: Compass Point Books, 2018.

INTERNET SITES

National Geographic Kids: Kids vs. Plastic
kids.nationalgeographic.com/explore/nature/kids-vs-plastic/

National Ocean Service: A Guide to Plastic in the Ocean
oceanservice.noaa.gov/hazards/marinedebris/plastics-in-the-ocean.html

TIME for Kids: The Problem with Plastics
timeforkids.com/g34/the-problem-with-plastic/

INDEX